TRAILBLAZERS OF THE WEST

THE TRANSCONTINENTAL RAILROAD

Tracks Across America

★ ★ ★

Jil Fine

HIGH
interest
books

Children's Press®
A Division of Scholastic Inc.
New York / Toronto / London / Auckland / Sydney
Mexico City / New Delhi / Hong Kong
Danbury, Connecticut

Book Design: Mindy Liu and Mikhail Bortnik
Contributing Editors: Eric Fein and Shira Laskin
Photo Credits: Cover © Hulton-Deutsch Collection/Corbis; p. 4 © Wolfgang
Kaehler/Corbis; p. 8 © Underwood & Underwood/Corbis; pp. 10, 14 © Corbis;
pp. 16, 18, 31, 33, 35, 36, 40 © Bettmann/Corbis; p. 23, Courtesy of The Bancroft
Library, University of California, Berkeley; pp. 24, 29 © Library of Congress
Prints and Photographs Division (HAER, CAL, 31-CISCO, 1-1, HAER, CAL,
31-DONPA, 1-3); p. 26 © Ron Thomas/Getty Images, Inc

Library of Congress Cataloging-in-Publication Data

Fine, Jil.
    The transcontinental railroad : tracks across America / Jil Fine.
    p. cm. — (Trailblazers of the West)
    Includes bibliographical references and index.
    ISBN 0-516-25128-7 (lib. bdg.) — ISBN 0-516-25098-1 (pbk.)
    1. Pacific railroads — Juvenile literature. I. Title. II. Series.

TF25.P23F56 2005
385'.0973 — dc22

                                                              2004021473

3 4 5 6 7 8 9 10 R 14 13 12 11 10 09 08   62

CONTENTS

INTRODUCTION

The sun beats down on your back. Sweat drips from your face. You pick up your heavy sledgehammer and drive another spike into the ground. The track boss yells, "Down!" and another rail is laid down in place. You will drive in many more spikes before your shift is over today. Your arms and back ache, but you feel proud because you know that you are making history. You are helping to build America's transcontinental railroad.

The transcontinental railroad was one of the greatest accomplishments of the nineteenth century. It crossed more than 2,000 miles (3,219 kilometers) of deserts,

◀ *The first transcontinental railroad brought together the east and west coasts of America. This is a model of one of the first engines to travel the tracks of the transcontinental railroad.*

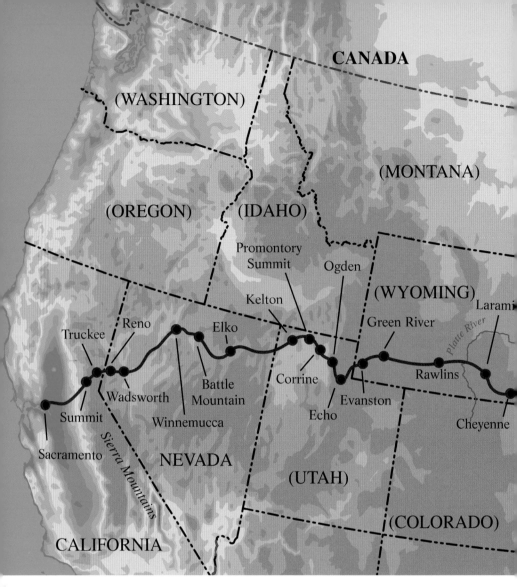

plains, rivers, and mountains. The railroad was the first connection between the east and west coasts of America. After the railroad was completed, a trip that once took months could take only a week. The building of America's first transcontinental railroad is a story of two

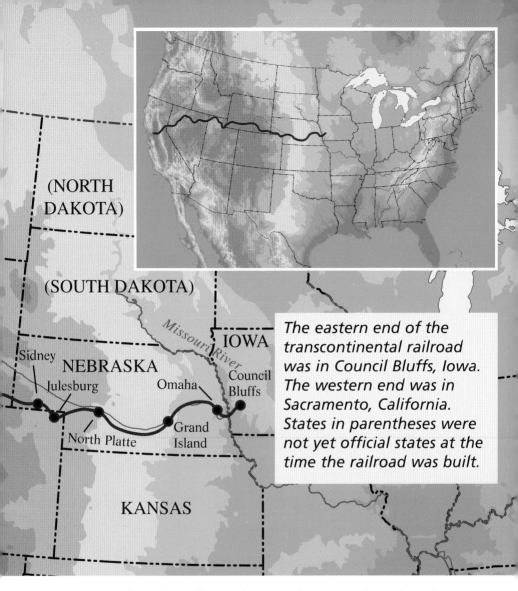

(NORTH DAKOTA)

(SOUTH DAKOTA)

Missouri River

IOWA

NEBRASKA

Sidney

Julesburg

Omaha

Council Bluffs

North Platte

Grand Island

KANSAS

The eastern end of the transcontinental railroad was in Council Bluffs, Iowa. The western end was in Sacramento, California. States in parentheses were not yet official states at the time the railroad was built.

teams of railroad workers who raced to finish their half of the railroad first. Let's hop aboard an "iron horse" and take a ride into the past to learn about the building of these tracks across America.

CHAPTER 1

A DREAM IS BORN

The Iron Horse

Up until the early 1800s, Americans mostly used horse-drawn carriages to move people and goods from place to place. In 1813, news arrived from England about a new form of transportation. This new type of transportation was a steam-powered locomotive that ran on tracks.

British engineers had used this locomotive to pull a wagon. Soon, American engineers were making steam-powered engines too. People became excited about the possibilities of steam-powered transportation.

◀ *On August 8, 1829, the first steam-powered engine in America was test-driven in Pennsylvania. People called the steam-powered locomotive the iron horse.*

The Dreamers

Some Americans came to believe that it would be possible to build a railroad across the United States. They thought that powerful locomotives would be able to pull many cars across this railroad system, which would run from coast to coast. In 1838, John Plumbe, an engineer, proposed the idea of a transcontinental railroad to the U.S. Congress. Congressmen laughed at Plumbe's idea, saying it was as silly as asking the government "to build a railroad to the moon."

Before the transcontinental railroad was built, people traveled across the country on horseback and in horse-drawn carriages.

The Rush Across America

Despite the congressmen's disapproval, the idea of a transcontinental railroad began to become popular. One reason for this was that many people wanted to settle in western lands. But to get there, they had to travel on dangerous wagon trails, or by sea around South America. Many died on the way. People needed a safer and faster method for traveling and transporting goods. Building a transcontinental railroad seemed to be the answer.

But there was much disagreement over where the railroad should be built and through which towns it should pass. People from the North wanted the railroad to pass through their states and the people from the South wanted it to pass through theirs. At this time, there was no plan for the location of the railroad. A decision would not be made for many years.

"Crazy" Ted Judah

Throughout the mid-1800s, railroads were being built up and down the East Coast. None, however, had been built west of the Missouri River.

In 1859, Theodore Judah, a successful engineer from the East, was in Sacramento,

California. Judah was there to build a short railroad line from Sacramento to the gold mines that were nearby. While in Sacramento, Judah became enthusiastic about the idea of a transcontinental railroad. Many people thought his idea was silly and called him "Crazy" Ted Judah.

Judah would not be discouraged. Like Plumbe, he went to Washington, D.C., to ask Congress to support a transcontinental railroad. Congress wanted to know how Judah's railroad would be able to cross the steep, dangerous Sierra Mountains in the West. Without a solution to the problem, Judah could not get the support of Congress. He returned to Sacramento to map out a practical, safe route to pass through the Sierras.

Dodge and Mr. Lincoln

Several other engineers were interested in a transcontinental railroad too. A young engineer named Grenville Dodge was measuring and mapping land west of the Missouri River in Council Bluffs, Iowa. In

August 1859, Abraham Lincoln, a candidate for the coming presidential election, met Dodge in Council Bluffs, Iowa. Lincoln asked him what the best route for a transcontinental railroad would be. Dodge replied that it would be best if the railroad went across the Platte River Valley.

Dodge thought that Council Bluffs would be a good place to start the railroad because it would be able to connect with railroads that already existed in Chicago, Illinois. Lincoln would later remember this conversation as president when he had to decide where the railroad would begin.

The Big Four

A year after he spoke with Dodge, Lincoln was elected president of the United States. Shortly after his election, in April 1861, the American Civil War began. By the early months of the war, Theodore Judah had found and mapped a way to travel safely across the Sierras. In June 1861, Judah and several other men, mostly rich investors, started the

Central Pacific Railroad of California. The four main investors in the Central Pacific were known as the Big Four. They were Collis Huntington, Charles Crocker, Leland Stanford, and Mark Hopkins. They, too, wanted to build a transcontinental railroad. In October 1861, Judah headed back East to convince Congress of his plan, which could make millions of dollars for his newly formed Central Pacific Railroad.

Collis Huntington (above) and Mark Hopkins were successful business partners who sold miners' supplies in California. Their money helped make the dream of a transcontinental railroad come true.

The Pacific Railroad Bill

After much hard work, Judah finally got congressional leaders to authorize the building of a transcontinental railroad. On July 1, 1862, Lincoln signed into law the Pacific Railroad Bill. In it, another railroad corporation was formed, called the Union Pacific. The Union Pacific was to start building westward from "a point on the western boundary of the State of Iowa." The Central Pacific was to build eastward from the Pacific Ocean coast to the eastern boundary of California. The companies would receive money and land grants from the government for each mile of track they completed. Judah and the Central Pacific got to work right away. On January 8, 1863, groundbreaking ceremonies were held in Sacramento, California.

After signing the Pacific Railroad Bill, President Lincoln still had to choose where the eastern end of the railroad would begin. In spring 1863, Lincoln asked Grenville Dodge, then serving as a general in the Union Army, where he would choose to start the railroad. Once again Dodge recommended the area near Council Bluffs, Iowa. President Lincoln agreed with Dodge. On December 2, 1863, groundbreaking ceremonies were held in Omaha, Nebraska, 2 miles (3.2 km) south of Council Bluffs. The enormous task of building a transcontinental railroad had begun.

CHAPTER 2

TRACKS ACROSS AMERICA

Moneymaking Schemes

Problems arose with the railroad before work even began. Some investors worried that they would not make enough profit on the running of the railroad. Some of them tried to increase their profits, sometimes illegally.

Peter Dey, head engineer for the Union Pacific, quit his job rather than go along with any illegal schemes. He did not want to be thought of as dishonest. Judah, who had become the Central Pacific's head engineer, also began to mistrust the way the Big Four wanted to do business. Instead of quitting, however, he tried to get other investors to buy the company from the Big Four.

In 1939, director Cecil B. DeMille made a movie about the construction of the transcontinental railroad called Union Pacific. *In this scene from the film, workers are laying down tracks to build the railroad.*

Judah's Final Trip

In October 1863, Judah left California for New York to talk to Cornelius Vanderbilt, a wealthy businessman. Judah hoped to get him to buy out the Big Four. However, Judah caught yellow fever on his trip. When he arrived in New York, his doctor could do nothing to help him.

On November 2, 1863, Judah died in New York. The Big Four gained complete control over the railroad. They hired a new head engineer, Samuel Montague, to replace Judah.

During the nineteenth century, many people died from yellow fever, a virus caused by a mosquito bite. This drawing, created in 1878, shows the terrible suffering caused by the disease.

General Dodge and the Union Pacific

Thomas Durant, the vice president and general manager of the Union Pacific, wanted to hire Lincoln's friend Grenville Dodge to replace Peter Dey. Dodge was widely known both as a skilled engineer and someone who had close relationships with powerful people in government. Durant hoped to take advantage of both. When the Civil War ended in 1865, Dodge agreed to join the Union Pacific.

Building the Railroad

Under Dodge's direction, Union Pacific workers became highly organized. Surveyors traveled ahead of all the other workers to properly map the route where the railroad would be built. After the surveyors came the graders. Graders flattened the ground for the laying of train tracks and built bridges and tunnels. Next came the men in the work gangs who put down the ties, laid the rails, and drove the spikes through the rails.

Because the land was already so flat in the East, the Union Pacific workers could lay track quickly. They often laid a mile or more of track in a day. The men were rewarded for their speed. Each man received two extra dollars in pay if he helped lay 2 miles (3.2 km) of track in one day.

Many workers were needed to build the railroad. Workers for the Union Pacific were mostly Irish immigrants or Civil War veterans. There were also many Germans, Englishmen, Native Americans, and African Americans working on the project. The men worked from sunrise to sunset. When they weren't working, many men drank liquor or gambled to pass their time.

Dance Halls and Casinos

As the railroad workers proceeded westward, businessmen followed. The businessmen built dance halls and casinos for the workers to spend their money in on their time off. The halls were canvas tents with wooden floors. They were about 100 feet (30.5 meters) long and 40 feet (12.2 m) wide. Workers danced as bands played music all night long.

DODGE IN THE ARMY

After fighting for the North in the Civil War, General Grenville Dodge led U.S. army forces against the Plains Indians. As the nation grew, the U.S. government tried to move Native Americans from their lands. In the Black Hills of South Dakota in September 1865, Dodge and his men came under attack from a group of Plains Indians. While escaping from them, he said, "If we can save ourselves, I believe we've found a pass through which the Union Pacific can go." A year later, he quit the army and became chief engineer of the Union Pacific.

Life on the Central Pacific

The Central Pacific had a harder time keeping their workers on the job. Many men left after payday to hunt for gold or other fortune. At the time, there were many Chinese men living in California. They, too, had come to seek their fortune in gold. Charles Crocker, one of the Big Four, wanted to hire some of these Chinese men to increase the number of workers. The construction foreman, James

Strobridge, refused to work with them. He thought the Chinese were too weak to do the job.

When there weren't enough white men willing to work for the Central Pacific, Strobridge agreed to let Crocker hire fifty Chinese men. They were paid less than the white workers and had to buy their own food. Yet the Chinese workers quickly changed Strobridge's mind. They worked hard and did not complain. Strobridge soon hired more Chinese workers. By the time the transcontinental railroad was completed, almost twelve thousand Chinese workers worked for the Central Pacific.

Blasting Through the Sierras
The Central Pacific's first task was to get through the Sierra Mountains. Workers had to dig tunnels and lay track through the mountain's tough granite stone. Work proceeded 24 hours a day. There were three shifts of workers and each man worked

8 hours. The work was very dangerous. Three men worked together to blast through the rock. One man held a drill in the rock while the other two hit it with 18-pound (8.2-kilogram) sledgehammers. After a hole was made, blasting powder was put into it and lit. The men ran

Thousands of Chinese workers took part in building the transcontinental railroad. This drawing of Central Pacific workers was featured in Harper's Weekly *magazine in 1867.*

from the explosion, hoping not to get hit with any flying rock. Once enough rock was broken, men would come in to clear it away. The men of the Central Pacific cleared only about 6 to 12 inches (15.2 to 30.5 centimeters) of rock each day.

Tunnels were made by using dangerous explosives to blast through rocky mountains.

Battling Mother Nature

Heavy snowfall during the winter of 1866 did not make work any easier for the men of the Central Pacific. Work slowed even more. Now the men had to tunnel through the snow to get to the underlying rock. The snow made the work even more dangerous. Explosions from the blasting powder sometimes set off avalanches. Many men were buried alive and their bodies were not found until the following spring. No one knows how many men died that winter while digging through the Sierras.

Native Americans and the Railroad

Workers for the Union Pacific faced their own dangers. These men had to deal with a problem Central Pacific workers in the Sierras did not have. That problem was angry Native Americans.

The U.S. government had taken or bought much of the land that had been the home and hunting grounds for thousands of Native Americans. With the coming of the railroad, more and more land was being taken from the Native Americans. Many were forced to live on reservations.

In response, many Native Americans raided the railroad camps, killed men, stole cows, bent the tracks, and did anything else they could to try to stop the railroad from being built. Some attempts were made to make peace between the railroad builders and the Native Americans, but with no success. The railroad men would not back down. They refused to stop their drive across America.

EAST COAST VERSUS WEST COAST

After the Tunnel

Central Pacific workers finished building their tunnels through the Sierra Mountains on November 30, 1867. While working through the Sierras, Central Pacific workers were only able to lay 12 inches (30.5 cm) of track a day. Outside the mountains, the workers' pace increased to 1 mile (1.6 km) a day.

Now that the slow work of tunneling through granite was over, a race between the Central Pacific and the Union Pacific was about to begin. The first company to reach the area of Ogden, Utah, would be able to set up a depot there to handle the tremendous amount of business from nearby Salt Lake City. Also at stake was who could win control of the land on which rich coal mines were located. Big money was on the line.

After Central Pacific workers finished the difficult job of building tracks through the Sierra Mountains (shown), they were ready to finish their end of the railroad.

Crocker and Strobridge did all they could to save time. To lay down track as quickly as possible, they avoided building bridges, making cuts into the earth, and other projects that took a lot of time. Much of the track ran in curves to avoid these projects. The Central Pacific was even able to collect more money from the government because the curves required more miles of track.

It often did not matter to either company how much anything cost or how well the track was laid. All that mattered to the leaders of the railroads was that they were getting the most money and land possible from the government.

The Home Stretch
By the end of 1868, the Central Pacific had laid 446 miles (717.8 km) of track from Sacramento, California, to Carlin, Nevada. By that time, the Union Pacific had laid 995 miles (1,601.3 km) of track from Omaha, Nebraska, to Evanston, Wyoming. Surveyors

To protect the tracks from being buried in the snow, the Central Pacific built large snow sheds over them. The longest snow shed was 28 miles (45.1 km).

and graders went miles ahead of the track layers, as sides pushed into Utah. As the winter of 1868 began, the competition was getting tough. In winters past, the Union Pacific workers had stopped work during snowstorms. This winter, however, the Central Pacific was racing across Nevada faster than ever, and the Union Pacific had to keep up. They worked all winter. Tracks were laid on snow and ice. Sometimes the snow was so deep that tracks were not put onto the ground. When the snow melted, the tracks would be left hanging in the air. This didn't matter to the Union Pacific though. They could fix things later, they thought. What mattered was winning the race at all costs. Through early 1869, the Union Pacific and the Central Pacific laid tracks across Utah. However, no final meeting place had been set by the government. The two routes were beginning to run parallel to one another! Yet neither company would stop building. In April, the U.S. government got involved.

Picking Promontory

President Ulysses S. Grant asked Grenville Dodge to meet with a representative of the Central Pacific to decide on a final meeting place for the transcontinental railroad. Dodge and Collis Huntington met. They decided that the tracks would meet in Promontory, Utah. The Central Pacific would buy track that the Union Pacific had already laid from Promontory to Ogden, which it would use as its own. The race was over.

Promontory, Utah, was the site of this wooden trestle. In this photo, workers are standing on cars being pushed by a locomotive.

The 10-Mile Day

Track still had to be laid for the two railroads to be joined in Promontory. A bet was made between Charles Crocker, one of the Big Four, and Thomas Durant, vice president of the Union Pacific. Durant bet Crocker that he and his men could not lay 10 miles (16.1 km) of track in one day. Crocker accepted the bet. On April 28, 1869, the men of the Central Pacific worked steadily for 12 hours, spiking 3,520 rails to 25,800 ties. When they were finished, they had laid 10 miles (16.1 km) and

56 feet (17.1 m) of track. The men got paid four times their regular daily wages. Durant never paid Crocker the ten thousand dollars he lost on the bet.

A Party in Promontory

On May 10, 1869, in Promontory, Utah, hundreds of people crowded around the tracks laid by the Central Pacific and the Union Pacific to celebrate the completion of the transcontinental railroad. The Big Four, Durant, Dodge, and Montague were there. Leland Stanford had brought several spikes, including a gold one to be put into the final rail. Stanford and Dodge gave speeches. After the speeches, Stanford placed the golden spike on the rail and swung his sledgehammer. To everyone's amusement, he missed and hit the rail. Durant then stepped up to swing the sledgehammer. He also

This monument at Promontory Point celebrates the driving of the last spike of the transcontinental railroad.

LAST SPIKE
COMPLETING FIRST
TRANSCONTINENTAL
RAILROAD
DRIVEN AT THIS POINT
MAY 10TH 1869

missed the spike. Finally, a railroad worker stepped in to save the day. He swung and hit the spike, joining the tracks and completing the transcontinental railroad.

·FRONTIER FACT·

When Leland Stanford attempted to drive in the golden spike, a telegraph operator standing by sent a telegram to let the world know that the transcontinental railroad was complete. The telegram was only one word—"Done."

After the gold spike was finally driven into the rail, a Central Pacific train, *Jupiter*, and a Union Pacific train, No. 119, were moved along the tracks toward each other. Dodge and Montague reached out from the front of each train and shook hands. The Central Pacific and the Union Pacific lines were joined.

People across America rejoiced when they heard the news that the transcontinental

After the last tracks of the transcontinental railroad were laid, a Union Pacific train from the East and a Central Pacific train from the West pulled up toward one another in celebration.

railroad was finished. Parades and parties were held in most major cities in America. The dream of building a transcontinental railroad had come true.

CHAPTER 4

ON THE TRAIN

Riding the Rails

Regular train service on the transcontinental railroad started on May 15, 1869. Many Americans had been eagerly waiting for the transcontinental railroad to be finished.

Thousands of people boarded the iron horse in the East for the eight-to-ten-day trip to the West. Luxury cars, called Pullman Palace cars, featured meals, electric lighting, lamps with silk shades, and heating and air-conditioning systems. First-class berths cost one hundred dollars from Omaha, Nebraska, to Sacramento, California. Today, that would be about thirteen hundred dollars! Second-class seats were seventy-five dollars, equal to about $990.00 today, and third-class seats cost forty dollars, about $525.00 today.

◀ *Luxury cars made long trips a pleasure for passengers who could afford to ride in them.*

The third-class cars were much different from the Pullman Palace cars. As many as ninety people were crammed into each car. The cars only had hard, wooden seats. Despite this discomfort, many people made the trip. They were going west for the promise of a better life. Railroad companies did all they could to get more people to go west. They needed workers and wanted to sell the millions of acres that they had gotten as land grants from the government. The railroad's efforts paid off. People flocked from Europe and the East Coast to settle in the West. Towns and cities grew around the railroad. The population of the West increased quickly.

·FRONTIER FACT·

The first reported train robbery on the Central Pacific railroad took place in Verdi, Nevada, on November 5, 1870. Five men armed with guns stole $41,600 in gold coins. Police chased robbers through two states before catching them.

From Coast to Coast
The railroad also helped the American people to prosper. Trade within the United States almost doubled. The American economy grew tremendously as the cost of transporting goods fell. Now people could sell their products to others across the country quickly and cheaply. People across the country were connected and able to trade goods and ideas with ease. America became more united overnight.

The Native American Way of Life
The railroad brought growth and prosperity to many people. Yet for some Americans, the transcontinental railroad had quite a different impact. As the railroad brought more people to the West, Native Americans were pushed farther from the lands they lived on. Those who refused to live on reservations were considered enemies of the United States. There were often battles between army troops

For centuries, Native Americans hunted on the lands that the transcontinental railroad would run through.

and these Native Americans. Thousands of Native Americans died as a result. The settlers that came west also hunted the buffalo to near-extinction. Native Americans used the buffalo as their main source of food, clothing, and shelter. With little land of their own and the absence of buffalo to hunt, the Native

American way of life was largely destroyed. We can only wonder what the fate of Native Americans would have been without the coming of the railroad.

While we may not know what life could have been for the Native Americans, we do know that the transcontinental railroad brought many positive changes for America. It helped the country grow as settlers moved west to build homes and businesses. The speed of mail delivery increased greatly and the cost of sending mail went down. New telegraph lines along the railroad allowed messages to be delivered in seconds.

The story of building the transcontinental railroad is an important part of America's past. What began as the dream of a few men became one of the greatest accomplishments in American history.

NEW WORDS

authorize (**aw**-thuh-rize) to give official permission for something to happen

avalanches (**av**-un-lanch-ez) large amounts of snow, ice, or earth that suddenly move down the side of a mountain

berths (**burths**) places to sit or sleep on a train

blasting powder (**blast**-ing **pou**-dur) an explosive material that is used to break up rock and other solid objects

casinos (ka-**see**-noz) places where people play cards and other games for money

depot (**dee**-poh) a railroad station

engineers (en-juh-**nihrz**) people trained to design and build machines, vehicles, bridges, roads, or other structures

foreman (**for**-mihn) a person in charge of a group of workers

graders (**grayd**-erz) people who level ground

granite (**gran**-it) a hard, gray rock

groundbreaking ceremonies (**ground**-bra-king **ser**-uh-moh-neez) celebrations marking the beginning of work on a project

immigrants (im-uh-gruhnts) people who come from abroad to live permanently in another country

investors (in-vest-ors) people who put money in a company with the hope of making more money

schemes (skeemz) plans or plots for doing something

spike (spike) a large, heavy nail often used to fasten rails to railroad ties

surveyors (sur-vay-ors) people who determine the best route for a road to travel over a piece of land

tie (tye) a brace that supports a railroad track, often made of wood

transcontinental (trans-kon-tuh-nen-tal) across a continent

trestle (tress-uhl) a framework that supports a bridge or railroad track

veterans (vet-ur-uhnz) people who have served in an army

FOR FURTHER READING

Durbin, William. *The Journal of Sean Sullivan: A Transcontinental Railroad Worker: Nebraska and Points West, 1867.* New York: Scholastic Incorporated, 1999.

Evans, Clark J. *The Central Pacific Railroad.* Danbury, CT: Scholastic Library Publishing, 2003.

Kalman, Bobbie. *The Railroad.* New York: Crabtree Publishing, 1999.

Magram, Hannah Straus. *Railroads of the West.* Broomall, PA: Mason Crest Publishers, 2002.

Murphy, Jim. *Across America on an Emigrant Train.* Boston, MA: Sagebrush Educational Resources, 2003.

Winslow, Mimi. *Loggers and Railroad Workers.* Brookfield, CT: Twenty-First Century Books Incorporated, 1997.

Organizations

Museum of Transportation
3015 Barrett Station Road
St. Louis, MO 63122
(314) 965-7998
www.co.st-louis.mo.us/parks/mot-museum.html

National Railroad Museum
2285 South Broadway
Green Bay, Wisconsin 54304
(920) 437-7623
www.nationalrrmuseum.org

RESOURCES

Web Sites

American Experience: Transcontinental Railroad
http://www.pbs.org/wgbh/amex/tcrr/
This Web site has lots of information and interactive activities on the transcontinental railroad.

California State Railroad Museum
http://www.csrmf.org
Learn about the transcontinental railroad, the gold rush, railroads in California, and more on this informative Web site.

Central Pacific Railroad Photographic History Museum
http://www.cprr.org
View interesting pictures and learn more about the Central Pacific's role in building the transcontinental railroad on this Web site.

INDEX

INDEX

About the Author

Jil Fine is the author of more than one hundred books for children and is a member of the Society of Children's Book Writers and Illustrators.